Katharine Tynan

Ballads and Lyrics

Katharine Tynan

Ballads and Lyrics

ISBN/EAN: 9783744775410

Printed in Europe, USA, Canada, Australia, Japan

Cover: Foto ©Thomas Meinert / pixelio.de

More available books at **www.hansebooks.com**

BALLADS AND LYRICS.

BY THE SAME AUTHOR.

SHAMROCKS.
Small crown 8vo.   5s.

"Written with simplicity, tenderness, and intensity of feeling."—*Academy.*
"Touches of true grace and distinction."—*Pall Mall Gazette.*
"Full of gorgeous colour and rich music."—*Truth.*

LOUISE DE LA VALLIÈRE, and other Poems.
Small crown 8vo.   3s. 6d.

"Sweet, pure, and high poetry."—*Truth.*
"Of no little merit."—*Academy.*
"Very seldom is it our good fortune to close a volume of poems with such an almost unalloyed sense of pleasure, and gratitude to the author.—*Graphic.*

A NUN: Her Friends and Her Order.
A Sketch of the Life of Mother Mary Xaveria Fallon.
With Portrait, crown 8vo.   5s.

"A prose poem, enriched by exquisite sketches, simple girlish sports, and womanly tenderness."—*Athenæum.*
"Exquisite prose idyll."—*Truth.*

LONDON: KEGAN PAUL, TRENCH, TRÜBNER & CO., LTD.,

Paternoster House, Charing Cross Road, W.C.

BY

KATHARINE TYNAN

Author of "Shamrocks," "Louise de la Vallière," &c.

"God's in His Heaven,
All's right with the World."

LONDON

KEGAN PAUL, TRENCH, TRÜBNER & CO., Ltd.

PATERNOSTER HOUSE, CHARING CROSS ROAD

1891

TO

ROSA GILBERT
(ROSA MULHOLLAND)

GREETING!

APOLOGIA.

*Here in my book there will be found
No gleanings from a foreign ground:
The quiet thoughts of one whose feet
Have scarcely left her green retreat:
A little dew, a little scent,
A little measure of content,
A robin's song, perchance to stir
Some heart-untravelled traveller.*

*A low horizon hems me in,
Low hills with fields of gold between,
Woods that are waving, veiled with grey,
A little river far away,
Birds on the boughs, and on the sward
Daisies that dancing praise the Lord.*

Outside my window I can see
The bent boughs of an apple-tree,
Where little fruits turn rosier;
And every evening of the year
I watch the golden sunsets die
Yonder in the wide Western sky.

The doves are crooning wild and soft,
Where elm and beech stand up aloft,
Houses of birds that build and fly.
The wind is the birds' lullaby,
Rocking small cradles to and fro,
As a fond mother's foot might go

And in my garden, all in white,
The Mary-lilies take the light,
And southern-wood and lavender
Welcome the bee, in golden fur
A splendid lover, and on high
Hovers the spangled butterfly,
Where roses, old and sweet, dream on,
Fading to rich oblivion.

And in my thatch the birds will build,
And still for me the sunshine gild
The world, though it be Winter day.
The rain will seem upon the spray

But showers of jewels, and the rime
Pale splendours raise in Winter time.

So in my book there will be found
No gleanings from a foreign ground.
If such you seek, go buy, go buy
Of some more travelled folk than I.
Kind Master Critic, say not, please,
How that her world so narrow is,
Since here she warns expectant eyes
That homely is her merchandise!

CONTENTS.

	PAGE
APOLOGIA .	vii
THE CHILDREN OF LIR .	1
SHEEP AND LAMBS .	6
ONLY IN AUGUST .	8
NIGHTINGALE .	10
OF AN ANGEL .	12
CUCKOO SONG	14
LUX IN TENEBRIS .	16
KINGS' PRISONERS .	17
AT ERCILDOUNE .	18
THE BLACKBIRD .	21
SECOND SIGHT .	23
A NEW OLD SONG	26
TO ROSE IN HEAVEN	28
A LED FLOCK .	31
WINTER EVENING .	32
IN A CATHEDRAL .	34
GOLDEN WEED .	36
OF ST. FRANCIS AND THE ASS	38
THE FAIRY BABE .	41

CONTENTS.

	PAGE
A Day-dreamer	43
Storm-gold	44
The Charity of the Countess Kathleen	45
A Girl's Lament	51
Home Sickness	53
Moods	55
De Profundis	57
Rain Raineth	59
To Inishkea	60
St. Francis and the Wolf	62
On a Birthday	68
The Death-watch	70
Our Lady's Exile	72
The Fairy Foster-mother	74
Michael the Archangel	77
Blackbird	79
Prince Connla of the Golden Hair	80
Over Mountains	84
Queen's Roses	86
The Witch	88
A Ring of Polycrates	90
Swallow	91
The Wild Geese	92
Of St. Francis: His Wrath	94
The Beloved	97
"In White Garments"	99
Green Gravel	101
The Dead Mermaiden	103
Rain in May	108
The Dead Son	109

	PAGE
GOLDEN LILIES	111
HOUSE-BUILDING	113
A WOMAN	114
THE DREAM OF MARY	116
A FRANCISCAN SERMON	117
SIGN MANUAL	120
THE HIDING-AWAY OF BLESSED ANGUS	121
THE LAST WORD	127
FAIRY HORSES	129
AUX CARMÉLITES	131
VOTIVE OFFERING	133
A STAR'S IMAGE	135
RAINY SUMMER	137
THE CHAPEL OF THE GRAIL	139
ALL IN ALL	143
TWO IN HEAVEN	146
IN IONA	148
ALL SOULS' NIGHT	150
RONDEAU	152

BALLADS AND LYRICS.

THE CHILDREN OF LIR.

"And their stepmother, being jealous of their father's great love for them, cast upon the King's children, by sorcery, the shape of swans, and bade them go roaming, even till Patrick's mass-bell should sound in Erin,—but no farther in time than that did her power extend."—*The Fate of the Children of Lir.*

Out upon the sand-dunes thrive the coarse long grasses,
    Herons standing knee-deep in the brackish pool,
Overhead the sunset fire and flame amasses,
    And the moon to eastward rises pale and cool:
Rose and green around her, silver-grey and pearly,
    Chequered with the black rooks flying home to bed;
For, to wake at daybreak birds must couch them early,
    And the day's a long one since the dawn was red.

On the chilly lakelet, in that pleasant gloaming,
    See the sad swans sailing: they shall have no rest:
Never a voice to greet them save the bittern's booming
    Where the ghostly sallows sway against the West.

"Sister," saith the grey swan, "Sister, I am weary,"
　Turning to the white swan wet, despairing eyes;
"Oh," she saith, "my young one," "Oh," she saith,
　　"my dearie,"
　Casts her wings about him with a storm of cries.

Woe for Lir's sweet children whom their vile step-
　　mother
　Glamoured with her witch-spells for a thousand
　　years;
Died their father raving—on his throne another—
　Blind before the end came from the burning tears.
She—the fiends possess her, torture her for ever.
　Gone is all the glory of the race of Lir;
Gone and long forgotten like a dream of fever:
　But the swans remember all the days that were.

Hugh, the black and white swan with the beauteous
　　feathers,
　Fiachra, the black swan with the emerald breast,
Conn, the youngest, dearest, sheltered in all weathers,
　Him his snow-white sister loves the tenderest.
These her mother gave her as she lay a-dying,
　To her faithful keeping, faithful hath she been,
With her wings spread o'er them when the tempest's
　　crying
　And her songs so hopeful when the sky's serene.

Other swans have nests made 'mid the reeds and
    rushes,
  Lined with downy feathers where the cygnets sleep
Dreaming, if a bird dreams, till the daylight blushes,
  Then they sail out swiftly on the current deep.
With the proud swan-father, tall, and strong, and
    stately,
  And the mild swan-mother, grave with household
    cares,
All well-born and comely, all rejoicing greatly:
  Full of honest pleasure is a life like theirs.

But alas! for my swans, with the human nature,
  Sick with human longings, starved for human ties,
With their hearts all human cramped in a bird's stature,
  And the human weeping in the bird's soft eyes,
Never shall my swans build nests in some green river,
  Never fly to Southward in the autumn grey,
Rear no tender children, love no mates for ever,
  Robbed alike of bird's joys and of man's are they.

Babbled Conn the youngest, "Sister, I remember
  At my father's palace how I went in silk,
Ate the juicy deer-flesh roasted from the ember,
  Drank from golden goblets my child's draught of
    milk.

Once I rode a-hunting, laughed to see the hurly,
    Shouted at the ball-play, on the lake did row,
You had for your beauty gauds that shone so rarely:"
    "Peace," saith Fionnuala, "that was long ago."

"Sister," saith Fiachra, "well do I remember
    How the flaming torches lit the banquet-hall,
And the fire leapt skyward in the mid-December,
    And amid the rushes slept our staghounds tall.
By our father's right hand you sat shyly gazing,
    Smiling half and sighing, with your eyes a-glow
As the bards sang loudly all your beauty praising:"
    "Peace," saith Fionnuala, "that was long ago."

"Sister," then saith Hugh, "most do I remember
    One I called my brother, you, earth's goodliest man,
Strong as forest oaks are where the wild vines clamber,
    First at feast or hunting, in the battle's van.
Angus, you were handsome, wise and true and tender,
    Loved by every comrade, feared by every foe:
Low, low, lies your beauty, all forgot your splendour:"
    "Peace," saith Fionnuala, "that was long ago."

Dews are in the clear air, and the roselight paling,
    Over sands and sedges shines the evening star,
And the moon's disk lonely high in heaven is sailing,
    Silvered all the spear-heads of the rushes are,—
Housèd warm are all things as the night grows colder,
    Water-fowl and sky-fowl dreamless in the nest:
But the swans go drifting, drooping wing and shoulder
    Cleaving the still waters where the fishes rest.

SHEEP AND LAMBS.

All in the April evening,
    April airs were abroad,
The sheep with their little lambs
    Passed me by on the road.

The sheep with their little lambs
    Passed me by on the road;
All in the April evening
    I thought on the Lamb of God.

The lambs were weary, and crying
    With a weak, human cry.
I thought on the Lamb of God
    Going meekly to die.

Up in the blue, blue mountains
    Dewy pastures are sweet
Rest for the little bodies,
    Rest for the little feet

But for the Lamb of God,
   Up on the hill-top green,
Only a Cross of shame
   Two stark crosses between.

All in the April evening,
   April airs were abroad,
I saw the sheep with their lambs,
   And thought on the Lamb of God.

ONLY IN AUGUST.

Only in August I have not seen you.
    August comes with his wheat and poppies;
    Ruddy sunlight in corn and coppice;
Only in August I have not seen you.

Autumn beckons far-off like a greeting.
    I and Autumn have secrets of you,
    All the Winter was long to love you;
Wintry winds have a song of meeting.

Dear is Summer, but Spring is dearer.
    In the Spring there was heavenly weather;
    Love and sunshine and you together.
Dear is Summer, but Spring is dearer.

June is fled with her rose and pansies.
    More is gone than a drift of roses,
    More than the may that the May uncloses,
More than April—with songs and dances.

Only in August I have not seen you.
>   Every month hath its share of graces,
>   Flowers, and song, and beloved faces.
Only in August I have not seen you.

NIGHTINGALE.

I have not seen you, I have not heard you,
    O, Nightingale, your silver woods among,
Pouring the passionate love and pain that stirred you
    Into a sudden heaven of heavenly song.
The dews around you, and the burnished moon above
       you,
    Below you the great trunks of forest trees.
Your immemorial lovers, they that love you
    Through nights and days and years and centuries.

What are you singing, glamouring voice of moon-tide?
    All loves that loved since Eden's lovers wed,
The joy and hope of youth before the noon-tide,
    The tears and pain, the peace that kissed the dead.
O, you have caught into your magical numbers
    All music Earth's musicians seek and miss;
The perfect picture Raphael saw in slumbers,
    The song Keats dreamed of that was never his.

I wish you came, O, scornful King of Singers,
    In early Summer to this hospitable land!
Honey-sweet is it while the Maytime lingers,
    With honeysuckles large as any hand.

With cowslips in the croft and in the meadow,
    With fairies dancing on the dewy moss and fern,
O, Nightingale, your bower of moon and shadow
    Waits for you, and our woodlands yearn and burn.

Are many gardens waiting long your coming
    And many lilies steeped in scented dew,
And in green aisles rich airs of Summer roaming
    And hearts of roses vaguely sad for you.
And songs our song-birds will be wild to lavish
    As flowers before you: they will dream awake
All night to hear your songs that sweetly ravish;
    The world will lie all sleepless for your sake.

OF AN ANGEL.

Never alone upon my way,
Mine Angel's with me every day,
And all night long he sits and sings,
Shaking the darkness off his wings.

The wavering moonlight steals and slips
From amber head to pinion tips,
Bathing him in a silver sea
That makes his eyes a mystery.

When I am bruised and sad and sore,
Have I not felt him leaning o'er,
Kissing my heavy lids to sleep?
Yea, I have heard him weep and weep.

In the noon-sun I see him stand,
Rosy azaleas in his hand;
His sapphire gown, his aureoled curl,
His opal wings and mother-o'-pearl.

And while this Angel walks with me
I fear not all the ill I see,
Though in the fruit a canker grows,
And serpents harbour 'neath the rose.

In noon-day gold, in moonlight snow,
I know the precious things I know,
Hidden not from my love-keen sight
By dazzle of day and mirk of night.

Mine Angel's praying hands and meek,
The pure young outline of his cheek,
His grave young mouth, his brow like snow,
His everlasting eyes I know.

Love lights his taper at those eyes,
O, stainless Bird of Paradise!
Love in your heart to Love divine
Has built a temple and a shrine.

O lips that bless, and eyes that yearn,
And sometimes sad, but never stern,
Dearest, my friend, my gift of God,
Companion on my dangerous road.

Stay with me, though the day be long,
And Heaven is lonelier for your song;
Though I be sad, and all my plea
Is only my soul's poverty.

CUCKOO SONG.

Cuckoo, cuckoo!
In April skies were blue
As every hedgerow knew;
And there was you.
In April
The cuckoo shows his bill,
With windflowers on vale and hill.
  O, Love!
Sweet was April, sweet was April!

Cuckoo, cuckoo!
In May his song was true,
And the world was new
For me and you.
In May
He sings all day,
All the long night that's sweet with hay.
  O, Love!
Blithe was the May, blithe was the May!

Cuckoo, cuckoo!
Last June the roses grew
In many a place we knew,
I and you.

In June
He changes his tune.
A young man's fancy changes soon.
  O, Love !
Fleet was June, fleet was June !

Cuckoo, cuckoo !
His notes are faint and few,
The lily is dying too,
For the rose there is rue.
In July
Away will he fly,
His notes blown back from an empty sky.
  O, Love !
Sad was July, sad was July !

Cuckoo, cuckoo !
No more we listen to
The merry song we knew,
I and you.
In August
Go he must,
Love and lovers will turn to dust.
  O, Love !
Cold is August, cold is August !

LUX IN TENEBRIS.

At night what things will stalk abroad,
    What veilèd shapes, and eyes of dread!
With phantoms in a lonely road
    And visions of the dead.

The kindly room when day is here,
    At night takes ghostly terrors on;
And every shadow hath its fear,
    And every wind its moan.

Lord Jesus, Day-Star of the world,
    Rise Thou, and bid this dark depart,
And all the east, a rose uncurled,
    Grow golden at the heart!

Lord, in the watches of the night,
    Keep Thou my soul! a trembling thing
As any moth that in daylight
    Will spread a rainbow wing.

KING'S PRISONERS.

Love in his net hath taken us, and bound us,
    Hath pinioned hands and feet right fast within,
Our master's mesh of gold goes round and round us,
    Cunningly wrought, and fairy fine and thin,
        To hold us in.

O Love Divine, O larger Love, come take us,
    Weave Thy sweet net outside our house of love;
Prisoners of Love, O Love Divine, come make us,
    Caught in thy snares, and seeking not to rove
        Outside Thy Love.

AT ERCILDOUNE.

"Love, how long wilt thou delay?"
    Sighing saith True Thomas;
Leans his face, grown old and grey,
    To the window glass—
Holds his burning eyelids so
    To allay their smart.
"Love," he says, "the hours go slow,
    Break in twain my heart."

Peace falls on the little town
    As on a soul shriven;
A large moon is gazing down
    From a speckless heaven.
All the village sleeping sweet
    Till the cock shall crow,
But the Rhymer's weary feet
    Travel to and fro.

Sometimes down the corridors
    Comes the White Lady;
Stiff silks rustle on the floors,
    Little heed takes he;

Fall her ghostly tears like rain
  With a dreary sound ;
Heart s blood drops and makes no stain
  On the snowy ground.

Other men are sleeping well
  In their chambers white ;
His old pain intolerable
  Bids him watch all night
With such watchers from the dead—
  Pain that takes his breath ;
Yesterday a young maid said
  He was old as death.

Ah, in his love's fairy-land,
  Clad in grass-green silk,
With the king's ring on his hand,
  Steed as white as milk,
When his love-locks lit the wind,
  And he laughed in mirth,
Never his equal might be found
  On this labouring earth !

Old as death, yet not to die !
  Would that he might see
Hart and hind come pacing by
  From the Eildon tree,

With their large eyes full of light,
    And their coats of snow !
When this thing shall greet his sight
    He shall surely go.

But so long he keeps his watch
    Hope may well grow dim ;
Every wind that lifts his latch
    Seems a call to him
Every cry of dreaming dove
    In the woodlands dumb
Seems the sweet voice of his love
    Calling him to come.

Old and cold, and cold and old,
    Oh, that he might see
Hart and hind with shoes of gold
    From the Eildon tree ;
Hart and hind with message kind
    Long, long are ye tarrying ;
Winter waileth in the wind,
    Far away is spring.

THE BLACKBIRD.

(A new song with an old burden.)

There's a lark in the noon sky, a thrush on the tree,
And a linnet sings wildly across the green lea,
And the finches are merry, the cuckoos still call,
But where is my Blackbird, the dearest of all?

They may talk of their gold-crests, but if he were by,
With his hair like the velvet and liquid dark eye,
What yellow-haired Saxon or Dane might compare
With my honey-voiced Blackbird, and the night on
    his hair?

There were many would love him, with beauty and
    wealth;
At the dance and the hurley, love-looks went by
    stealth
From blue eyes and brown eyes: he saw only me.
God bless my bold Blackbird, wherever he be

When I went out a-walking the fields were all green,
With a wide drift of sunshine, and daisies between,
And the birds sang at building, but tears made me blind
For my Blackbird of April, so handsome and kind.

Oh, if we were building our nest, I and he,
With my voice for his pleasure, and his song for me,
I would sing all the summer, and make the birds mad,
For the love of my Blackbird, the one love I had!

SECOND SIGHT.

"Sister," said blind Dara,
   "What do you behold?"
Round her and St. Brigid
   Flowed the dawn's gold.
"Sister," said blind Dara,
   "Would that I might see
Veils of gold and silver
   Drawn on hill and lea!"

Over her and Brigid
   Carolled the lark;
Hills were heights of Heaven,
   Though their feet were dark.
Dew in the shadow
   Pearled the gossamer;
Kine in the meadow
   'Gan to low and stir.

Mists from the bogland
   Curled like silver smoke,
Young birds were singing
   In the arching oak.
To the east and southward
   Scarlet grew the world,
And the sun leapt upward,
   As a ball is hurled.

Brigid, lost in praying,
   Touched her sister's eyes;
"Oh," she said, "my sister,
   Dove of God, arise!
Eyes no longer sightless,
   See His glory spread!"
Dara, with a loud cry,
   Lifted up her head:

Saw the little rivers
   Glide through bogland brown,
Where the yellow iris
   Flaunted her go'd gown:
Saw that sea of scarlet
   Flush on hill and wood;
Praised God's name, rejoicing
   That His works were good.

"Yet," she said, "my sister,
   Blind me once again,
Lest His presence in me
   Groweth less plain.
Stars and dawn and sunset
   Keep till Paradise,
Here His face sufficeth
   For my sightless eyes."

"Oh!" she said, "my sister,
  Night is beautiful,
Where His face is shining
  Who was mocked as fool.
More than star and meteor,
  More than moon or sun,
Is the thorn-crowned forehead
  Of the Holy One."

"Haste," she said, "and plunge me
  Once again in night,
Lest perchance I lose Him,
  Gaining my sight."
Brigid, lost in praying,
  Touched her eyes once more,
And the light went fading
  Off sea and shore.

All His creatures praise Him,
  From daylight to dun,
Stars and moon and cloudland,
  And Messer the Sun;
Seas and hills and forests,
  And the frozen waste:
Dara in her blindness
  Praiseth Him best.

A NEW OLD SONG.

The Spring comes slowly up this way,
   Slowly, slowly!
A little nearer every day.

The blackbird's trilling shrill and gay
His roundelay and virelay;
Good lack, as though the March were May!

In kirtle all of green and grey;
   Slowly, slowly,
The Spring comes slowly up this way!

She hath delicious things to say,
But will not answer yea or nay,
Nor haste her secrets to display.

The Spring comes slowly up this way,
   Slowly, slowly!
To make the world high holiday.

The pink is on the orchard spray,
The lambs put off their fears and play,
Gone are the snows of yesterday.

'Twere well if Spring might always stay !
      Slowly, slowly,
The Spring comes slowly up this way.

TO ROSE IN HEAVEN.

ROSE KAVANAGH.
(*Died February* 26, 1891.)

I.

My Rose, 'twas the wild rose you were,
    Trailing upon the hedgetop green;
    No narrow garden hemmed you in.
You had the dearest face, my dear,
    Rose and white with a touch of brown,
    Sweet as the country come to town.

The children found your goodness out,
    The old folk and the poor and weak,
    And the dog's instinct wise and quick.
To me, my dear, in pain and doubt
    What were you? Ah, well, none can take
    The empty place that is heart-break.

The bravest eyes that ever were
    You had; the honest heart and mind,
    The tolerant judgment large and kind.
Dear, in some day of pain and care,
    How we shall miss your eyes and face!
    And oh, your Heaven's a far-off place.

II.

You need not fear again
   The east wind and the snows,
Nor dree your weird of pain,
   Sickness and dying, Rose.
In God's land summer is,
And health and youth and bliss.

You need not go away,
   When going was like death,
For leave to live your day,
   For leave to draw your breath.
In God's land where you are,
Sweet is the summer air.

You need not have for friend,
   Housemate and wayfarer,
Pain that had never an end,
   And sickness hard to bear;
Or lie the long night through
While life ebbed out from you.

Oh! *there* is no home-sickness,
   Because it is our home;
Nor labour nor distress,
   Nor watching wearisome.
You need not fear the snows,
North wind or east wind, Rose!

III.

I hope you will not wear in Heaven
    A different face from that we knew,
Rose, like the rose that morn and even
        Hath sun and dew !

Wear no new smiles, but smile as when
    You were our own, to heal and bless,
Drawing from heavy hearts of men
        Their heaviness.

Be just so kind, be just so brave
    There in your glory infinite !
No primrose growing on your grave
        Is half so sweet

As you, my dear, were in the world.
    You leave your own place desolate,
The pale spring foliage is uncurled
        And the birds mate

The pleasant days you loved of yore.
    I think that where you are, my dear,
You love the things you loved before
        When you were here.

Wear no new face, but keep the old,
    Look from your glory and your grace,
From underneath the rays of gold
        With the old face !

A LED FLOCK.

Who keeps this flock of waves like sheep
    Crested and curled as white as curds?
"I," saith the Lord, "this great flock keep,
    Yea, it obeys My lightest words."

O Lord, but yesternight this flock,
    So innocent seeming in the sun,
Roared like wild beasts, and on the rock
    Gored the drowned mariners every one.

"But even then," the Lord replied,
    "The flock was Mine, and in such wrath
I gathered trembling to My side
    The victims withered in its path.

"Oh, if their mothers could but see
    The estate of them the wild waves slew,
Then they would say, beholding Me,
    'The sea is His great Angel too!'"

WINTER EVENING.

But the rain is gone by, and the day's dying out in a splendour,
    There is flight as of many gold wings in the heart of the sky:
God's birds, it may be, who return from their ministry tender,
    Flying home from the earth, like the earth-birds when darkness is nigh.
Gold plumes and gold feathers, the wings hide the roseate faces,
    But a glimmer of roseate feet breaks the massing of gold:
There's gold hair blowing back,—and a drifting of one in clear spaces,
    A little child-angel whose flight is less sure and less bold.

They are gone, they are flown, but their footprints have left the sky ruddy,
    And the night's coming on with a moon in a tender green sea,

And my heart is fled home, with a flight that is certain
    and steady,
  To her home, to her nest, to the place where her
    treasure shall be.
Across the dark hills where the scarlet to purple is
    waning;
  For the birds will fly home, will fly home, when the
    night's coming on.
But hark! in the trees how the wind is complaining
    and straining,
  For the birds that are flown it may be, or the nests
    that are gone.

IN A CATHEDRAL.

Up in the roof the carver wrought,
   Creating many a lovely thing;
His hand's true service shaped his thought,
   He toiled to please no crownèd king,
But the dear Christ whose image dim
Gazed from the tall rood under him.

Patiently, oh, patiently,
   His flowers unfolded from the wood;
His fruit grew on the long-dead tree;
   His elves took life, a sportive brood;
He fashioned many a singing-bird
Whose lovely silence praised the Lord.

He made a row of vines in fruit,
   And peaches on a southern wall,
And here a sad and stringless lute
   With dulcimers unmusical,
And roses red and lilies white,
And stars that lit no heaven at night.

His woodland creatures gazed at you
   Out from old boughs with lichen sere;
And flying birds that never flew
   Soared in the summer dusk up here,
Where a young angel prayed and smiled,
For all his wings a human child.

The patient carver toiled apart;
   The world roared on – a world away.
No earthly ties were round his heart,
   No passion stirred his quiet day;
His carvings in the cloister dim
Made home, and wife, and child to him.

He was so young when he began—
   A fair-haired boy, whose wistful eyes
Saw earth and heaven, and scarcely man,
   But weighed large issues and were wise:
The years that all unheeded sped
Shook their grey dusts upon his head.

And when this wilderness of shade,
   Far from men's eyes, made God's heart glad,
He woke from dreams, and, undismayed,
   Knew he was old, and cold, and sad;
He kissed his nerveless good right hand,
And died—his name was writ in sand.

GOLDEN WEED.

Buttercup is golden,
    Gold is a star,
But the yellow bindweed
    Is goldener far.

Gold was the crocus,
    Like a gold cup
That the King's handmaiden
    Stately lifts up.

Gold was the daffodil
    When the winds blow;
And the white daisy
    Gold heart will show.

Gold is the reaping,
    And the great moon:
Gold was the yellow-bill
    Singing in June.

Though all the west sky
  Is flecked to gold flame,
Still my brave yellow weed
  Puts it to shame.

Dappling the wayside
  Burnt up and brown,
Till it is cloth of gold
  For the Queen's gown.

Queen, you have gold hair
  Like a gold veil,
But the gold bindweed
  Turns your gold pale.

OF ST. FRANCIS AND THE ASS.

Our father, ere he went
   Out with his brother, Death,
Smiling and well-content
   As a bridegroom goeth,
Sweetly forgiveness prayed
   From man or beast whom he
Had ever injurèd,
   Or burdened needlessly.

"Verily," then said he,
   "I crave, before I pass,
Forgiveness full and free
   From my little brother, the ass.
Many a time and oft,
   When winds and ways were hot,
He hath borne me cool and soft,
   And service grudged me not.

"And once did it betide
   There was, unseen of me,
A gall upon his side
   That suffered grievously.
And once his manger was
   Empty and bare, and brown.
(Praise God for sweet, dry grass
   That Bethlehem folk shook down!)

"Consider, brethren," said he,
   "Our little brother; how mild,
How patient, he will be,
   Though men are fierce and wild.
His coat is grey and fine,
   His eyes are kind with love;
This little brother of mine
   Is gentle as the dove.

"Consider how such an one
   Beheld our Saviour born,
And carried Him, full-grown,
   Through Eastern streets one morn.
For this the Cross is laid
   Upon him for a sign.
Greatly is honoured
   This little brother of mine."

And even while he spake,
    Down in the stable stall
His little ass 'gan shake
    And turned its face to the wall.
Down fell the heavy tear;
    Its gaze so mournful was,
Fra Leo, standing near,
    Pitied the little ass.

That night our father died,
    All night the kine did low:
The ass went heavy-eyed,
    With patient tears and slow.
The very birds on wings
    Made mournful cries in the air.
Amen! all living things
    Our father's brethren were.

THE FAIRY BABE.

(A LULLABY.)

Between the night and the grey morning,
When lights are out and the crickets sing,
The fairies stole my bud and my blossom
And laid this wizened thing in my bosom.
   Hush, O!
  Sleep, little fairy, sleep,
  Dream of the fields and the sheep,
  But never a sorrowful dream may take you
  Of the mother that could forsake you.
   Hush, O!

My little boy was rosy and sweet,
I kissed him over from head to feet;
But cold hands came in the midnight lonely
And drew him off, O my one child only.
   Hush, O!
  Sleep, little fairy, sleep,
  Sleep while I wake and weep,
  For it may be my little son misses
  The mother's milk and the love and kisses.
   Hush, O!

The fairy-woman, with magic skill,
Came full of charms to work you ill;
I stood up in a sudden anger
And caught you into my breast from danger.
   Hush, O!
 Sleep, little fairy, sleep,
 All that I have to keep;
 For on your face that is pinched and weary
 I saw a look of my own, own dearie.
   Hush, O!

My boy that went in the wild morning
Shall wear a crown and a gay gold ring,
Shall ride a splendid horse when he's older,
With cloak of velvet upon his shoulder.
   Hush, O!
 Sleep, little fairy, sleep,
 Stars are beginning to peep,
 And may your mother my wee son cherish
 That so he go not milkless and perish
   Hush, O!

A DAY-DREAMER.

Since coming from the land of dreams is lonely,
    And the world's daylight very cold and grey,
I will return beyond the sun's rim only,
    Into the gold dusk of my yesterday,

I will return through yonder purple coppice,—
    But O, thou love-worn nightingale, be still!—
Into a world of silken, scarlet poppies,
    Wherein who loveth dreams shall have his fill.

STORM-GOLD.

After the rainy day.
   After the stormy weather,
Breaks the gold in the grey,
   Gold and silver together.
Flutters and falls the splendour,
   Turns to scarlet and rose;
Clear in a sky that is tender
   A crescent-moon grows.

After the rainy day
   The passion and sobbing are over;
Dim in distance away
   Seem my love and my lover.
The gold of the evening is round me,
   Night comes with the wings of a dove;
The peace of the evening hath bound me
   Far sweeter than love.

THE CHARITY OF THE COUNTESS KATHLEEN.

O Countess Kathleen,
    Kathleen O'Hea!
She was grander than the Queen,
    The old people say.
She was like the Lady Mary
    In God's blessed Town,
With stars for her rosary,
    And sunlight for her gown.

Black fell potato blight
    On the kindly fruit;
Evil demons came by night,
    Withered flower and root.
And the corn-ears never filled,
    And the sun grew dark;
All the floods of heaven were spilled,
    And we had no ark.

O Countess Kathleen,
    Kathleen O'Hea !
You're a Saint—a Saint and Queen,
    The old people say.
And while you pray, so still and pale,
    With gold hair to your feet,
The powers of hell will sure avail
    Against Christ Jesus, sweet.

There are come in the town
    Merchantmen twain ;
Dark are they, of renown,
    Have sailed many a main.
With gold fillets on their hair,
    And gold in their hands,
They buy a merchandise most rare,
    The rarest in all lands.

O Countess Kathleen,
    Men's souls they buy.
You are richer than the Queen,
    And the poor folk die.
God's image creeps and craves,
    And the world's a hearse ;
If the corpse-light lit our graves,
    We were scarcely worse.

She hath sold her house and lands,
　　Gold cups and gear,
And a fleet of ships is manned,
　　Bringing food and cheer.
But a storm arose ere day,
　　By the power of hell;
And the ships in Blacksod Bay,
　　Half-wrecked, rose and fell.

O Countess Kathleen,
　　Kathleen O'Hea!
Jesus Christ in Heaven, I ween,
　　Goeth sad to-day.
All the shepherds dead or fled
　　Who that flock did keep;
Jesus asks in voice of dread:
　　"Where are My sheep?"

She stepped out of her castle-door
　　Like a dead Saint;
And her feet scarce touched the floor,
　　And her eyes were faint.
Past the market-cross and well,
　　Swiftly she came,
Heard the toll of the death-bell,
　　Ever the same.

O Countess Kathleen,
    Kathleen O'Hea!
She was like the marble Queen
    In the Abbey grey.
Past the people she is gone,
    Up the inn stair,
In the chamber, all alone,
    Where the demons were.

They were counting up their store,
    Littling its worth.
Now who standeth in the door?
    Flower of all the earth,
With her white soul in her hand,
    Fair beyond desires;
And her eyes like theirs who stand
    In eternal fires.

O Countess Kathleen,
    Kathleen O'Hea!
Heard them chaffer, shrill and mean,
    Let them say their say,
But this soul, so white of hue,
    Jesus Christ held dear;
It was worth all souls, they knew,
    They could gather here.

Thus she bought the bartered souls,
  Emptied their pack,
She hath gathered up the scrolls,
  Each man hath his back.
Now those merchantmen are fled,
  And there's food to eat ;
All the starving folk are fed,
  Full with wine and meat.

O Countess Kathleen,
  Kathleen O'Hea!
Ullagone! and raise the keen !
  Cold and dead she lay.
O ye folk, at what a price
  She hath ransomed
Poor men's souls for Paradise,
  With her own instead !

O Countess Kathleen,
  Kathleen O'Hea !
She was like the lilies' queen,
  The old people say.
On her breast the white lilies,
  On the dusky pall ;
But the Cross she dared not kiss,
  Turned against the wall.

*   *   *   *

Praised be the Lord Jesus!
　　Could He forget
How she sold her soul for us,
　　Paying our debt?
Swiftly His Messenger
　　Doeth His behest;
And that gentle soul they bear,
　　Even to His breast.

But that day was Satan wroth,
　　And his fury fell
On the accursed traders both,
　　Traffickers of hell.
They, below the river bed,
　　In great chains are caught,
Till they have deliverèd
　　That dear soul they bought.

O Countess Kathleen,
　　Kathleen O'Hea!
For her charity, I ween,
　　High she sits to-day.
Roses grow about her feet,
　　The rose in her hair,
Because Love's flower is found most meet
　　For her to wear.[1]

A GIRL'S LAMENT.

(TO AN OLD BURDEN.)

I WISH I were like yonder gull
That fills the whole grey twilight full
With flapping of wings and crying dull,
   All in the winter gloaming, O.

For then I'd fly with wings of grey
Over the sea and far away,
Seeking my lover, brave and gay—
   'Tis he that's long of coming, O.

I put my apron over my head,
I cried till both my eyes were red:
I knew it was my heart that bled.
   The skies are always raining, O.

I cannot spin, I cannot churn;
No more the griddle-cakes I turn;
Cusha is lowing in the barn—
   'Tis she that is complaining, O.

But will you not come back, come back?
My cheeks are pale, my breath is slack;
And you may get a suit of black,
   And court another lover, O.

And I shall wear a shroud of lawn
With many a posy strewn thereon.
Ah, woe! I fear you're dead and gone,
   For you were never a rover, O.

HOME SICKNESS.

Sometimes in the evening,
   When the mountains are grey,
I muse on mine own country
   That's far, far away.
O there are white palaces
   By a jasper sea!
And I trow mine own country
   Is the best land for me.

Green are the fields thereof,
   Spangled with gold.
Glad goeth many an one,
   Stricken of old.
Old friends and lovers,
   Dead long ago.
Smiling and greeting,
   Whiter than snow.

Yonder the sky's yellow,
    And rosy and green,
With drift of angels' feathers
    And gold harps between.
And I think if I might travel
    Where the gates open wide,
I should see mine own country
    Lie smiling inside.

Come ye, all my beloveds,
    Rise up by cockcrow,
For our own country calls us,
    And we have far to go!
And were any left in exile,
    That bitter pain to dree,
Ah, even mine own country
    Would be exile to me!

MOODS.

Yesterday, or a year ago,
I heard the arid East wind blow;
There was no joy in flower or tree,
No bird's song came to comfort me,
No shade was in the blinding sky,
The parched grass shivered audibly,
The West at evening held no star;
Even mine angel seemed far;
There was no freshness in the morn,
I rose forlorn and slept forlorn.
Yesterday, or a year ago,
My heart went fasting after feast,
With the wind in the East.

This eve or any eve at all
The blue South wind is musical.
Through my low garden gate I see
The Western glories facing me,
God's flower of fire that grows not cold.
My lilac's black against the gold,
The splendour of light unspeakable;
Yea, and my blackbird singeth well;

The dewy garden's drenched with scent,
My soul hath measureless content
This eve or any eve at all;
Thanksgiving in my heart and mouth,
With the wind in the South.

DE PROFUNDIS

You must be troubled, Asthore,
   Because last night you came
And stood on the moonlit floor,
   And called again my name.
In dreams I felt your tears,
   In dreams mine eyes were wet;
O, dead for seven long years!
   And can you not forget?
   Are you not happy yet?
     The mass-bell shall be rung,
     The mass be said and sung,
     And God will surely hear;
     Go back and sleep, my dear!

You went away when you heard
   The red cock's clarion crow.
You have given my heart a sword,
   You have given my life a woe,

I, who your burden bore,
    On whom your sorrows fell;
You had to travel, Asthore,
    Your bitter need to tell,
    And I—was faring well!
       The mass-bell shall be rung,
       The mass be said and sung,
       And God will surely hear;
       Go back and sleep, my dear!

RAIN RAINETH.

There are diamonds hung on the spray,
And sea-fog blown from the bay,
    The world's as wet as a river,
    O thrush, sing now, or sing never,
        Spring seems far away.

Sing out, O blackbird, my king,
My heart is sick for the Spring,
    And O, the drenching grey weather
    With April half through her tether,
        And May on the wing!

For I think when the hawthorn blows,
And the lily's in bud, and the rose,
    Perhaps one would scarcely remember
    To grieve for a day of November;
        ——But nobody knows!

TO INISHKEA.

I'll rise and go to Inishkea,
Where many a one will weep with me
The bravest boy that sailed the sea
  From Blacksod Bay to Killery.

I'll dress my boat in sails of black,
The widow's cloak I shall not lack,
I'll set my face and ne'er turn back
  Upon the way to Inishkea.

In Arran Island, cold as stone,
I wring my hands and weep my lone
Where never my true love's name was known :
  It were not so in Inishkea.

The friends that knew him there will come
And kiss my cheek so cold and numb.
O comfort is not troublesome
  To kindly friends in Inishkea !

'Tis there the children call your name,
The old men sigh, and sigh the same ;
'Tis all your praise, and none your blame,
    Your love will hear in Inishkea.

But you were dear to beast and bird,
The dogs once followed at your word,
Your feet once pressed the sand and sward—
    My heart is sore for Inishkea.

I'll rise and go to Inishkea
O'er many a mile of tossing sea
That hides your darling face from me.
    I'll live and die in Inishkea !

ST. FRANCIS AND THE WOLF.

This wolf for many a day
   Had scourged and trodden down
   The folk of Agobio town ;
Old was he, lean and grey.

Dragging a mildewed bone,
   Down from his lair he came,
   Saw in the sunset flame
Our father standing alone.

Dust on his threadbare gown,
   Dust on his blessed feet,
   Faint from long fast and heat,
His light of life died down.

This wolf laid bare his teeth,
   And growling low there stood ;
   His lips were black with blood,
His eyes were fires of death.

So for a spring crouched he;
   But the Saint raised his head—
   "Peace, Brother Wolf," he said,
"God made both thee and me."

And with the Cross signed him:
   The wolf fell back a-stare,
   Sat on his haunches there,
Forbidding, black, and grim.

"Come nearer, in Christ's Name,"
   Said Francis, and, so bid,
   Like a small dog that's chid,
The fierce beast fawning came,

Trotting against his side,
   And licked the tender hand
   That with soft touch and bland
Caressed his wicked hide.

"Brother," the Saint said then,
   "Who gave thee leave to kill?
   Thou hast slain of thine own will
Not only beasts but men.

"And God is wroth with thee:
   If thou wilt not repent,
   His anger shall be sent
To smite thee terribly.

"See, all men hate thy name,
   And with it mothers fright
   The froward child by night :
Great are thy sin and shame.

"All true dogs thee pursue ;
   Thou shouldst hang high in air,
   Like a thief and murderer,
Hadst thou thy lawful due.

"Yet, seeing His hands have made
   Even thee, thou wicked one,
   I bring no malison,
But blessing bring instead.

"And I will purchase peace
   Between this folk and thee,
   So love for hate shall be,
And all thy sinning cease.

"Say, wilt thou have it so ?"
   Thereat, far off, we saw
   The beast lift up his paw,
His great tail wagging go.

Our father took the paw
   Into his blessed hand,
   Knelt down upon the sand
Facing the creature's jaw.

That were a sight to see :
   Agobio's folk trooped out ;
   They heard not all that rout,
Neither the beast nor he.

For he was praying yet,
   And on his illumined face
   A shamed and loving gaze
The terrible wolf had set.

When they came through the town,
   His hand that beast did stroke,
   He spake unto the folk
Flocking to touch his gown.

A sweet discourse was this :
   He prayed them that they make
   Peace, for the Lord Christ's sake,
With this poor wolf of His ;

And told them of their sins,
   How each was deadlier far
   Than wolves or lions are,
Or sharks with sword-like fins.

Afterwards some came near,
   Took the beast's paw and shook,
   And answered his sad look
With words of honest cheer.

Our father, ere he went,
    Bade that each one should leave
    Some food at morn and eve
For his poor penitent.

And so, three years or more,
    The wolf came morn and even,
    Yea, long forgiven and shriven,
Fed at each townsman's door;

And grew more grey and old,
    Withal so sad and mild,
    Him feared no little child
Sitting in the sun's gold.

The women, soft of heart,
    Trusted him and were kind;
    Men grew of equal mind,
None longer stepped apart.

The very dogs, 'twas said,
    Would greet him courteously,
    And pass his portion by,
Though they went on unfed.

But when three years were gone
    He came no more, but died
    In a cave on the hillside;
You may count each whitening bone.

And then it came to pass
 All gently of him spake,
 For Francis his dear sake,
Whose Brother Wolf this was.

ON A BIRTHDAY.

Shall I lament my vanished spring?
Ah no, its joys went withering:
Its hopes, long sick, decayed and died
With its desires unsatisfied:
A moaning wind of discontent
Stripped the young boughs of bloom and scent;
The rain was raining every day.

Now though it be no longer May,
Oh heart, what youth renewed is ours!
With generous scarcely hoped-for flowers.
And the good summer but begun:
With longer days and riper sun,
And the large possibilities
Of gifts and grace and good increase
In the rich weather yet to come.

Nor shall the autumn strike us dumb
Who knows what fruit for us shall be
Swung in some ruddy-hearted tree;
What hopes shall find their harvesting

When outward birds are on the wing;
When pale September lights her fire—
Her Will-o'-the-Wisp on every briar—
What ship shall sail to shore at last?

Nor shall we dread the winter blast
Or the long evening of our year
With nothing more to hope or fear:
Looking to keep Christ's festival,
In His own fair and lighted hall.
After the longest night is done,
Cometh the Christmas benison.

THE DEATH-WATCH.

Ullagone! Ullagone!
He and I were all alone.
In the wall by the thatch
I heard the tick of the death-watch.

Ullagone! Ullagone!
And my heart grew cold as stone:
Tick, tick, all was still
Save that ghastly note of ill.

On the flaring candle grew
Plain an awful shape I knew:
Tick, tick, in the thatch
Went the beat of the death-watch.

Ullagone! Ullagone!
And the tide went with a moan.
Bring the candles, two and three;
Chant the dead man's litany.

Strew the rose, the rosemary gather
For the husband and the father:
Tick, tick, in the thatch
Hear the knell of the death-watch!

OUR LADY'S EXILE.

Twelve years, and down on earth the time was long:
    She was dreaming all alone in her leaf-framed bower,
    What time the limes and almonds were in flower;
Outside the casement was a white bird's song
      Ringing and clinging; there was scent of spice
      From some far opening door in Paradise.

About her were magnolias, white and red,
    And palms like emerald flame went leaping up
    From the poor setting of an earthen cup,
Lilies grew pale, and roses crimsonèd:
      At dawn a little angel like a child
      Brought them to her, and kissed her gown, and smiled.

Such heavenly visitants were often here,
    For this one brought her flowers, and that one fruit;
    And here one sitting tinkled to his lute,
Singing the songs the Lord Christ loves to hear;
      And there one floated in the gathering gloom,
      Like a flushed lily or a rose in bloom.

Across the sun His birds, the cherubim,
    Went flying home like distant flakes of light,
    And a late lark was scaling heaven's blue height,
Seeking to trace the self-same path to Him;
    Then the sun setting caught her robe's white fold,
    And lit her mournful eyes with sudden gold.

"How long," she sighed. If but the door would swing,
    And Michael enter in his silvery mail,
    And the plumed helmet, where the ringed stars pale,
And glow about his curled hair glittering,
    And lean to her, and place the torch a-lit
    In her tired hands that ofttimes longed for it.

No sign! the red hearts of the roses burned
    Love-lit; a fiery moon was in the sky,
    And the night wind was trembling like a sigh;
Faint and far-off the ringdoves yearned and mourned,
    And from the olives came a voice forlorn,
    That bird who leans her heart upon a thorn.

THE FAIRY FOSTER-MOTHER.[2]

Go not into the meadow, Ailie,
    Under the June moon!
Fairies in the shadow, Ailie,
    Croon a sad tune,
And their great King is sad, Ailie,
    With his head into his hands,
For his delicate little lad, Ailie,
    Far off in fairy lands.

He thinks on his dead wife, Ailie,
    And heaves many a sigh.
She gave her babe her life, Ailie,
    And never said good-bye.
And the little son like silk, Ailie,
    Is dwindling every day
For mother's love and milk, Ailie,
    Ailie, come away!

Run home, Ailie asthore,
   To your own little one!
Your husband stands at the door,
   And shades his eyes from the sun,
And calls you home from the cows
   Ailie, his pride and joy,
Star of the home and house,
   To the fine husband and boy!

Her smile was strange and still,
   She held her eyelids down;
She went by the ruined mill
   By the ragweed yellow and brown,
Into the field forlorn,
   With fairy rings on the ground;
In the gloom of the fairy thorn
   Were fairies circling around.

She is gone on the fairies' horse
   The ragweed, yellow and sly,
She will be a fairy's nurse
   And wipe the tear from his eye;
And her own wee troublesome lad
   May pine, and she will not come:
Her husband be crazed and sad,
   But she will never come home.

Never, never again, Ailie,
    Though long we look for you,
Never in sun or rain, Ailie,
    Never in dusk or dew.
With your night-black hair like silk, Ailie,
    And your eyes like the sky,
And your skin as white as milk, Ailie
    Ailie Carroll, good-bye!

MICHAEL THE ARCHANGEL.

Not woman-faced and sweet, as look
The angels in the picture book;
But terrible in majesty,
More than an army passing by.

His hair floats not upon the wind
Like theirs, but curled and closely twined;
Wrought with his aureole, so that none
Shall know the gold curls from the crown.

His wings he hath put away in steel,
He goes mail-clad from head to heel;
Never moon-silver hath outshone
His breast-plate and his morion.

His brows are like a battlement,
Beautiful, brave, and innocent;
His eyes with fires of battle burn—
On his strong mouth the smile is stern.

His horse, the horse of Heaven, goes forth,
Bearing him to the South and North,
Neighing far off, as one that sees
The battle over distances.

His fiery sword is never at rest,
His foot is in the stirrup prest;
Through all the world where wrong is done
Michael the Soldier rideth on.

Michael, Commander! Angels are
That sound the trumpet, and that bear
The banners by the Throne, where is
The King one nameth on one's knees.

Angels there are of peace and prayers,
And them that go with wayfarers,
And them that watch the house of birth,
And them that bring the dead from earth,

And mine own Angel. Yet I see,
Heading God's army gloriously,
Michael Archangel, like a sun—
Splendid beyond comparison!

BLACKBIRD.

Though Christmas boughs were green in bud,
   And hoodwinked flowers began to show;
The blackbird grew not warm in blood:
   And when the Spring comes he will know.

For all the sky's soft, shining fleece,
   And winds that from the southward blow,
My wise heart Blackbird held his peace:
   And when the Spring comes he will know.

To-day the unquiet wind is chill,
   The steely sky is charged with snow;
But Blackbird's singing with a will:
   And when the Spring comes he will know

The sea-fog's blowing from the east,
   But thoughts of birds on nesting go;
And Blackbird's singing of a feast:
   And when the Spring comes he will know.

PRINCE CONNLA OF THE GOLDEN HAIR.

Prince Connla of the Golden Hair,
    All day he goeth listlessly;
    From the first dawn to sunset sky
He goeth like a sleep-walker.
For his old sport he hath no care,
    His steed is idle in the stall,
    His hounds are sleeping, one and all,
The rust his armour-plates will wear.

On a tall throne his father is,
    The hero of the Hundred Fights.
    Now his old dreams are sad o' nights
For his son's moon-struck fantasies;
So fair, for any queen to kiss,
    So brave, so strong, so wise in youth,
    That was a sorry hour, in truth,
That slew the Kingdom's hope like this.

Last night he heard the banshee grieve,
    Outside his walls incessantly—
    If for his own death grieved she,
He would not go so sad this eve,
For life is not too sweet to leave;
    But his young son whose heart will break
    Just for a phantom lady's sake.
'Tis a vile net some witch doth weave.

The Druid comes and stands by him,
    Wise words may give the young Prince peace.
    Lo! then a voice that will not cease,
Sweeter than any vesper hymn,
Sweeter than choirs in forests dim,
    Rises upon the enamoured air,
    With an old melody, wild and fair;
Prince Connla leaps in heart and limb,

And flushes, and his eyes are glad;
    He knows the words the song will say:
    " O my true lover, come away
To my bright land where nought is sad
From all those grieving doubts you had;
    Where sickness cometh not, nor care,
    Nor age to wither the gold hair,
Nor tears, nor Death that maketh mad."

"Far in the west," she saith, "it lies,
 Gold pastures by a sapphire sea;
 Our palace-towers stand silvery
Against the rose and amber skies.
There too our shadowy gardens rise,
 With fruit and flowers like jewels set,
 Where a brown nightingale singeth yet,
And lovers whisper lovers' sighs."

He hears, and sees her standing there,
 A slim shape in her gown of silk,
 Threaded with pearls as white as milk.
One scarlet rose she hath to wear,
Flaming against her shoulder bare.
 She takes his hand in hers a while,
 Drawing his heart out with her smile,
Prince Connla of the Golden Hair.

The King and Druid standing by
 Are grieved, there's nought to see at all,
 Save a tree's shadow on the wall.
But hush!—Prince Connla suddenly,
With half a smile and half a sigh;
 "A burden is an earthly crown,
 A burden, and I lay it down,
And I go lighter till I die."

Then by that shape invisible,
    He's gone down the long forest aisle;
    Flames the great sunset many a mile,
The goldenest sunset ever fell,
Thrilling with light incomparable
    The sea-world and the startled land.
    Lo there, a shallop by the sand,
Rocked, like a rainbow-tinted shell.

Crystal it was, with green and rose
    Shot in it, like the irised dove;
    A great bird at the prow thereof,
Flapped his wide wings like Arctic snows,
And chains of silver, fine and close,
    Bound bird and boat inseparably.
    To a gold rose grew sky and sea
Where the rich colour ebbs and flows.

And in that strange enchanted air,
    The lovers stepped aboard and went
    Sailing to that lost Continent,
Over the leagues of clear water.
But the King, standing spell-bound there,
    Groaned, his great heart was rent in twain.
    And never an eye beheld again
Prince Connla of the Golden Hair.

OVER MOUNTAINS.

My heart went roaming and flying
   Where her one treasure was.
The East was luridly dying,
   A low wind sobbed, "Alas!"

There was no bird at all
   Out of its nest so warm;
Over the mountain wall
   My heart went into the storm.

And when the night was mirk,
   And on the shrieking sea
The wind was doing its work,
   My heart came back to me.

Tapped at my window-pane.
   Out of the storm and din,
Out of the night and rain,
   I rose and let her in.

O, heart, like a frightened bird,
    Heart like a small grey dove,
Say hast thou seen or heard
    Anything of our love?

But never a word she said,
    Her eye was leaden and dim,
Her breast had a stain of red,
    She spake no word of him.

And whether she saw him not
    Over the mountains grey,
Or whether he had forgot,
    I know not to this day.

QUEEN'S ROSES.

Sweet St. Elizabeth, 'tis said,
Once when the beggars would be fed,
   All in a fold of her gown's gold
Went carrying them the wheaten bread.

But the King met her angrily;
Half-white, half-red with wrath was he,
   Stung for her sake, that she should take
The scullion's duty, even she,

The sweetest woman under the sun.
He laid both hands her shoulders on;
   Looked like a sword, but spake no word
The Queen's tears, gathering, down did run;

Her gown slipped from her trembling hold,
And lo! not bread was in its fold,
   Out then there fell, O miracle!
Roses the loveliest, red and gold.

   *   *   *   *

Roses for bread, the story saith :
Some day, O my Elizabeth
   You will go down in your gold gown,
And where the crowned King tarrieth :

And in your gold gown's fold shall be
The white bread of your charity ;
   " Even as you fed the hungerèd,
You did the like to Me," saith He.

Then your gold gown let down shall show
The loveliest roses ever ablow,
   For bread, God's roses white and red,
That in His garden grow a-row ;

Roses that take you with their breath.
Yet go not, my Elizabeth.
   For while you stay in dark and day
God's Rose lights up this world of death.

THE WITCH.

Margaret Grady—I fear she will burn—
Charmed the butter off my churn;
'Tis I would know it the wide world over,
Yellow as saffron, scented with clover.

At Omagh market the witch displayed it:
Ill she had gathered, ill she had made it.
Hid in my cloak's hood, one glance I threw it,
Passed on smiling; my troth! I knew it!

Sheila, the kindest cow in the parish,
Mild and silken, and good to cherish,
Shame her own gold butter should leave her
To enrich the milk of a low-bred heifer!

I said not Yea or Nay to the mocker,
But called the fairy-man over from Augher;
Like a russet he is that's withered,
Bent in two with his wisdom gathered.

He touched the butter, he peered and pondered,
And crooned strange rhymes while I watched and
    wondered :
Then he drew me out through the gloaming
O'er the fields where the mist was coming.

He bewitched me so that I know not
Where they may grow, where they may grow not ;
Those witch-hazels he plucked and plaited,
Crooning on while the twigs he mated.

There's the wreath on the churn-dash yonder.
All the neighbours view it with wonder ;
And 'spite of Father Tom I avow it
The yield is doubled since that came to it.

I bless the fairy-man though he be evil ;
Yet fairy-spells come not from the Devil ;
And Margaret Grady—I fear she will burn—
I do forgive her, with hate and scorn.

A RING OF POLYCRATES.

BECAUSE that Fate was kind to me,
    I was afraid of my kind fate;
And flung my ring in the blue sea,
    Where now I stand and wait.
And storm and shine flit by apace
Over my jewel's resting-place.
The appeased gods dwell unansweringly;
It comes not back to me.

Now, am I blest, or am I curst?
    More sad or glad than the fabled king?
Sometimes I think Fate's best or worst
    Were naught against my ring.
My ring, my ring, that held alway
Its illumined heart by night and day!
Without it I am old and cold,
In ermine and in gold.

SWALLOW.

One swallow does not make a Summer.
    Proverbs are wise, you early swallow;
Yet the Spring's here with you, new-comer,
    April's here, and the May to follow,
May and June and the happy Summer.

O swallow that has never a fellow,
    Your home-sick heart grew tired of straying,
Of Eastern scarlet skies and yellow;
    And you were fain to go a-maying
Deep in home woods with Spring for fellow.

The blackbird sang long ere your coming:
    The thrush hath children under her bosom;
Yesterday there were brown bees humming
    Round and over the cherry-blossom.
Vagrant winds of the South were roaming.

Proverbs die, and their makers wither.
    You whom the proverb so dispraises,
Satellite of the golden weather,
    Loved of the children and the daisies,
Summer comes on your sea-blue feather!

THE WILD GEESE.

(A Lament for the Irish Jacobites.)

I HAVE heard the curlew crying
   On a lonely moor and mere;
And the sea-gull's shriek in the gloaming
   Is a lonely sound in the ear:
And I've heard the brown thrush mourning
   For her children stolen away;—
But it's O for the homeless Wild Geese
   That sailed ere the dawn of day!

For the curlew out on the moorland
   Hath five fine eggs in the nest;
And the thrush will get her a new love
   And sing her song with the best.
As the swallow flies to the Summer
   Will the gull return to the sea:
But never the wings of the Wild Geese
   Will flash over seas to me.

And 'tis ill to be roaming, roaming
  With the homesick heart in the breast!
And how long I've looked for your coming,
  And my heart is the empty nest!
O sore in the land of the stranger
  They'll pine for the land far away!
But Day of Aughrim, my sorrow,
  It was you was the bitter day!

OF ST. FRANCIS: HIS WRATH.

Our father, 'spite his tenderness
    For all the dear God made,
    Certes, at times was not afraid
To ban as well as bless.

There was a young bird, ravening;
    A little lark this was;
    From a low nest in sunny grass
His parents rose to sing.

And in the nest as well as he
    Four young birds soft and sweet,
    Through dew, and dusk, and noontide heat
In love did well agree.

Thither our father often came,
    Rejoicing to behold
    God's little birds, with throats of gold,
Trembling to praise His Name.

And here he often stayed and prayed
    Deriving much pleasure,
    From the dear anthem wild and pure
The larks sang overhead.

And oftentimes he raised his hand,
    Blessing those little birds;
    Who piped in answer to his words,
As they could understand.

But this young lark of whom I tell,
    Content not with his share
    Of worms, and flies, and such like fare,
Cruel, insatiable,

Upon his little brethren set,
    And with his beak them slew.
    It chanced our father came thereto
While yet the blood was wet;

And saw the parents flying round,
    Their song all turned to moan;
    The murderer, careless, from a stone
Did view that slaughter-ground.

Our father's wrath and pity grew
    And kindled to a flame;
    " Ah, thou vile bird of woe and shame,
Ill fate will thee pursue!

"Miserably shalt thou die," he said,
    "Be drowned, for all thy wings;
    And loathed by all living things,
Even when thou art dead.

"The painted insect in the grass,
    The frog that croaks anigh,
    The firefly and the butterfly
Will hate thee as they pass.

"Even the cats and dogs," he said,
    "And carrion birds of air,
    On thy vile carcase will not fare:
A curse is on thy head."

And even so it came to pass.
    Before three days were done,
    That lark was drowned in a tank of stone,
The peacock's looking-glass.

And there he lay in Heaven's eye,
    Dead, and dishonoured too,
    Till someone passing by him threw
Upon a dunghill nigh.

Of all foul things in beast or bird,
    Or in men's hearts that be,
    This, the foul fiend of cruelty
Our father most abhorred.

THE BELOVED.

Blow gently over my garden,
    Wind of the Southern sea,
In the hour that my Love cometh
    And calleth me!
My Love shall entreat me sweetly,
    With voice like the wood-pigeon;
"I am here at the gate of thy garden,
    Here in the dawn."

Then I shall rise up swiftly
    All in the rose and grey,
And open the gate to my Lover
    At dawning of day.
He hath crowns of pain on His forehead,
    And wounds in His hands and feet;
But here mid the dews of my garden
    His rest shall be sweet.

Then blow not out of your forests,
    Wind of the icy North;
But Wind of the South that is healing
    Rise and come forth!
And shed your musk and your honey,
    And spill your odours of spice,
For one who forsook for my garden
    His Paradise!

"IN WHITE GARMENTS."

You were young and brave
    And fair in men's sight.
They streaked you for the grave
    In a garment of white:
Your smile was sweet, they said,
When you were lying dead.

And were you glad to go,
    O my heart, O my dear?
The North Wind brings the snow,
    And Winter's long down here;
And you are very far
In lands where roses are.

I yearned so for your sake
    Lying dead in your youth;
My heart was like to break
    For pity and for ruth:
And the world's a changed place
Without your eyes and face.

A young man clad in white.
  I think of him who told
The tidings of delight
  To the women of old :
" He is arisen again,"
O, Easter healeth pain !

A young man clad in white.
  " I am the Life," One saith
Who broke with hands of might
  The bitter bonds of death.
Amen ! Lord Jesus dear,
The Easter-time draws near.

Now summon from the dead
  This young man clad in white,
Like him who comforted
  The women by daylight.
Thy garden's fair to see—
Lord, let him walk with Thee !

There's a delicate time of hope
  When Easter comes and Spring,
And the pink buds will ope
  And birds begin to sing ;
But Winter's slow to go,
And the North Wind brings snow.

GREEN GRAVEL.

A CHILD'S RHYME.

Green gravel! green gravel! the grass is so green
For the prettiest young fair maid that ever was seen.
We'll wash her in new-milk, and clothe her in pink,
And write down her name with a gold pen and ink.

Her eyes are like diamonds, her hair is like wheat,
And her cheeks like the roses so dainty and sweet;
She'll have gowns of the velvet, and a gay golden comb,
And a ring on her finger, when her true love comes home.

Green gravel! green gravel! your true love sends word
That he dons all his bravest and buckles on his sword,
And is coming to wed you, so preen you up fine,
Set the music a-going, and flowing the wine.

Now he comes for to marry her, we'll dress her in
    white,
Sprinkled over with daisies so golden and bright,
And a veil of fine silver we'll throw on her hair,
Lest the roses grow envious and die of despair.

But where is he tarrying, the gallant bridegroom?
For the priest 's in the parlour, and the bride in her
    room.
And the bridesmaids have left her to sigh her soft
    sigh,
To her tears, and her smiling, and her mother's good-
    bye.

Green gravel! green gravel! your true love is dead,
And he sends you a message to turn round your head;
And to turn on your pillow with your face to the wall,
You're a maid and a widow and no wife at all!

Cold, cold in her bride-clothes she lay down so meek,
With her hands on her bosom and her hair by her
    cheek;
Now come, ye fine gentlemen, and bear ye the bride
Where her bridegroom is sleeping. Let them sleep
    side by side!

THE DEAD MERMAIDEN.

(FOR A PICTURE.)

ST. BRANDAN, coming out of his cell,
    On a wild morning,
Hears o'er the yellow ocean-swell
    The breakers sob and sing.

All rosy lie the beaten sands
    In the morning light;
Wide-winged, between the sky and lands
    A cormorant hangs in sight.

The sea-weeds heapèd dank and brown
    Are high and low;
Upon the sand-hills' shifting crown
    The drenched gulls sit a-row.

St. Brandan lifting up his hands
    In the new morning,
Praiseth the Lord of sea and lands;
    The breakers shrilly sing.

St. Brandan raising yet his hands,
    With reverent breath,
Prayeth for mariners of all lands
    Whom last night brought to death.

But what is this the waves bring close?
    Tossed to and fro—
This delicate thing of gold and rose,
    And whiter than the snow?

This thing of rose and snow and gold,
    Shaped fair withal?
Lost from the sea-king's palace cold?
    A mermaid such they call.

The kindly sea-weed drapes her fair
    Down from the waist;
The diamond sands are in her hair
    And sparkle on her breast.

He draws her in; his eyes are dim,
    His thoughts are faint;
This seems as sweet a thing to him
    As any savèd Saint.

As any Saint that brings him balm
    In a troubled hour,
Dorothy with her rose and palm
    Or Barbara with her tower.

He kneels him down; he needs must weep
    She looks so mild,
This half a creature of the deep
    And half a maiden-child.

Upon her closed eyes mild and meek
    The tears have dried,
The hues of death are in her cheek,
    The rocks have gored her side.

Sudden he lifts his hands above
    Prays with a cry:
Christ Jesus, the dear Lord of Love,
    Sits in His palace high.

Christ Jesus bends Him low to hear,
    And holds His breath:
"Now for true service many a year,
    A soul"—St. Brandan saith—

"A soul, a soul, my Master dear,"
    He prayeth still,
The tender Shepherd smiles to hear—
    His servant pleads not ill.

Nay, well as him who anciently
    Wrestled amain,
And would not let the angel be:
    Of blessing he was fain.

Sudden the mermaid opes her eyes,
    And " Jesus " saith,
But scarce might speak for windy sighs
    That strangle still her breath.

Yet " Jesus ! " saith and with the name
    Grows bright to see,
As though within her form a flame
    Doth burn up joyously.

St Brandan rises up from her
    And hasteneth where
A little pool of rain water
    Lies in the rock-face bare ;

And gathers in his hollow palm,
    And comes again,
And pours it on her forehead calm,
    The dew of Heaven's rain.

With Father, Son, and Holy Ghost
    Is baptism given ;
Never shall this dear soul be lost
    That preens its wings for heaven.

That taketh flight ; yea, even now
    The bird hath flown ;
St. Brandan with his hidden brow
    Is praying here alone.

He makes her grave in holy earth,
    In blessèd ground:
Of mourners there shall be no dearth,
    The grey gulls cry around.

The cormorant hangs no more anigh,
    He is fled home;
His little ones cry hungrily
    Fishing beside the foam.

The muddy breakers sigh to sleep,
    The moon is white;
In a sea-palace fathoms deep
    Are tears and death and night.

RAIN IN MAY.

O RAIN in May, and I recall
You and May and the evenfall;
   And every garden drenched and sweet,
   And the laburnum drowned in it;
The patter of rain is musical.

You and I in the wet May weather,
You and I and the Spring together.
   And in the long suburban road
   No other creature walked abroad.
Wildly sweet is the wet May weather.

And scarcely over land and sea,
And scarce in paradise might be
   Such joy, the while the blackbird trilled,
   His throat with musk and honey filled,
Songs of love from the lilac tree.

THE DEAD SON.

The boy was in the clay,
    The mother was weeping still
From dawn to evening grey
    When stars looked over the hill.
Between the dawn and dark,
    The night and day between,
About the stillest hour of mirk
    Oh, who is this comes in?

He did not lift the latch,
    He came without a sound,
He stood within a moonlit patch,
    A space of holy ground.
His robe was to his feet,
    All of the fair silk fine,
The gold curls were soft and sweet
    That she was used to twine.

But on his hair of silk
  There was a drift like rain,
His robe as white as milk
  Did show a piteous stain.
"O mother, mother!" he said,
  "Your tears have wet me through;
I am come from the blessèd dead
  To try and comfort you.

"The other children play,
  But when I would rejoice,
O mother, I hear from far away
  The crying of your voice!
Your tears are heavy as lead,
  I cannot run or leap;
O mother, mother, mother," he said,
  "I pray you not to weep!"

The red cock and the black
  Crew, and her lamb was gone;
She rose and set the window back
  And welcomed in the dawn.
She swept the sanded floor,
  And made the fire to burn,
With all her weeping done and o'er.
  God comfort them that mourn.

GOLDEN LILIES.

O Daffodils all aflame,
I know from whence ye came
To warm March with your blaze!
   As Gabriel went a-winging
Through flowering country ways,
   He heard your trumpets ringing.

God's Paradise this was,
With a city of rainbow glass,
The River of Life there flows,
   The Tree of Life there blooming
Hath many a name that glows
   Like flower and fruit illuming.

But Gabriel going down,
With a gold gown and crown,
Was grave as him bestead;
   Great tidings he was bringing,
To raise the earth from dead,
   And set the heaven to singing.

"Oh, young," he said, "is she,
God's Maid and Queen, Marie;"
He said, " I will bring down
   These golden trumpets blowing,
And lay them on her gown,
   To glad her with their showing."

Queen Marie in her bower
Had a white lily in flower,
And Gabriel brought the gold,
   The gold lily that ever
Blowing his trumpet bold,
   Declares her praise for ever.

HOUSE-BUILDING.

I'VE heard the mellow blackbird singing clearly
    Over the building of his wattled house,
Wherein some morn, when skies are rose and pearly,
    A small brown head shall bend to hear his vows.

I've seen the merry squirrel hoard his treasure
    Of milk-white nuts against a time of cold:
The little mate who shares his simple pleasure
    Hath eyes of amber and a fur of gold.

Oh, happy creatures, sweet is the providing,
    Sweet is the building of the little home!
Oh, sweet, I know, to gather up in hiding
    Treasures to deck the rooms where love shall come.

The light heart makes the hard work sweet and easy.
    Sweet is the time when all the world grows green,
And love puts off his splendours and is busy
    Building the house and decking it within.

A WOMAN.

As one might see an enchanted land
Mistily over sea and strand
Purple and gold on the sky-line,
And since he might not go would pine,
So is she, with her old joys dead,
Her rose of life all witherèd.

Nay, there is ripe gold on the wheat,
And the wind bids you welcome, sweet.
Are lilies in the garden bed,
And a lark singing overhead,
Mists of blue Summer, and aloft,
Ripe apples in the orchard croft.

She will not hear. She sees across
The world, with a sick sense of loss,
A house that none hath builded well,
A heaven wherein she shall not dwell,
A threshold that she may not pass.
Hearth-fires that none hath lit, alas!

Voices of children calling her
Mother, to make her heart-strings stir,
Are calling in that lonely house ;
Sweet as young birds the dawn will rouse,
The yellow heads against her knee
Flutter and dance untiringly.

And since one man will never come
And take her hand and lead her home
Opening the long-locked door for her,
The glory withers off the year,
Though she is patient : but to-day
Life goes for her a dusty way.

And for that music most forlorn,
Voices of children never born,
And the love words that are not hers,
Even the sweet sky choristers
Pleasure her not. Oh, let her be,
She and her dreams are company.

THE DREAM OF MARY.

(From the Welsh.)

"Mary, Mother, art thou asleep?"
  "Nay, dear Son, but waking and dreaming."
"Mary, Mother, why dost thou weep?"
  "I saw Thy dear Blood flowing and streaming."

"Mary, Mother, tell me thy dream."
  "Blessed Son, Thou wert trapped and taken,
Scourged with stripes in a hall didst seem,
  Mocked with laughter, despised, forsaken."

"Blessed Mother, thy dream tell all."
  "Blessed Son, on a Cross wert lying,
While a black, blind knave from the hall
  Pierced Thy heart that was warm from dying."

"Mary, Mother, thy dream is true;
  True thy dreaming, sad Mother Mary;
Whether the years be many or few
  Still the hunters gain on the quarry."

Over the hill, and a cold, cold hill,
  I saw Mary dreaming and weeping,
Making a space betwixt souls and ill,
  Snatching men from hell and its keeping.

A FRANCISCAN SERMON.

Little children, for His sake,
Who a baby's form did take,
Who disdainèd not at all
Asses' manger, oxen's stall,—
Love His dumb things for His sake.

From that stall at Bethlehem
His child's gaze was turned on them,
Very sweetly it might be
For their hospitality;
Inns were full at Bethlehem.

All the world went round and round,
Ignorant; might none be found
Worthy to behold His birth
Save those lowliest things of earth,
While the ignorant world went round.

Not by chance, O children dear.
Read His lesson; it is clear:
Not the lowliest living thing
Stands outside His fathering;
Read His lesson, children dear.

He, God's Lamb, and little Child,
Surely He was sweet and mild
As those innocent lambs you know,
Gambolling in their coats of snow;
Imaging God's Lamb and Child.

For His sake, the blessed Lamb,
Love dumb creatures in His Name,
Our poor brethren, patient, mild,
Lowlier than the lowliest child,
Ass and oxen, sheep and lamb.

And the dear birds of the air,
All their pretty nestlings spare;
And the fly upon the pane;
And the butterfly so vain
Of his wings that light the air.

Not alone your dog so wise,
With his kind heart in his eyes;
Nor your bird that sings in mirth;
Nor your pussy on the hearth,—
Love all living things likewise.

Let your love be wide as His,
With the whole world round His knees;
Gather into your warm heart
All His creatures,—not a part;
So your love shall be like His.

Save from want and cruelty
Things that walk and things that fly;
Make for them the world more sweet
By your coming into it;
Fight His fight 'gainst cruelty.

Oh, believe me, little ones,
Much a tender heart atones,
Making a child's heart like His:
He rejoices when He sees
Kindness in His little ones.

SIGN MANUAL.

This is Thy lamb, yea, Lamb of God,
   This, for whose sake Thy veins ran dry,
This, for whose sake by a hill-road
   Thou wentest forth to die.

This is Thy lamb, though torn, defiled
   By the beast's teeth. Where no stars gleam
All night, and never an angel smiled;
   It went in an ill dream.

So is it torn and stained so deep,
   Thy lamb, Thy lamb, bruised and astray.
Oh, the true Shepherd knoweth His sheep,
   Though hirelings turn away.

See then below the scarlet sin
   Shaming its heat, Thine own mark, see
Thy Name in blood that hath sunk in
   Dripping from Calvary Tree.

THE HIDING-AWAY OF BLESSED ANGUS.

(Ireland, A.D. 770.)

BECAUSE his fame was noised abroad
    And blown about from sea to sea,
Angus, God's singer, dear to God,
    Ate ashes in humility,
Deeming man's praise as nothing more
Than chaff upon a winnowing floor.

But since such dust might enter in
    And choke the soul, he fled away
One morning, when the birds begin
    About the time of gold and grey;
And came barefoot, with tattered gown,
To Tallaght, nigh to Dublin town.

At Tallaght the great Friary stood,
    A hive of very saintly bees.
Their Abbot, Melruan, wise and good,
    Angus besought on bended knees
Some task, however hard and rough,
Nor drive the starving beggar off.

His face was grimed with dust and sweat,
   His lips were at the threshold stone ;
His eyes with scalding tears were wet,
   He beat his breast with many a moan :
Surely, my Lord the Abbot thought,
Some sinner in whom grace hath wrought.

He sent him out to tend the kiln,
   To feed the mill and grind the corn.
Like a great clown of little skill
   He bore large burdens, night and morn.
He cleaned the cattle's house and laid
The food before each grateful head.

Yet still he sang, lest God should miss
   One voice that praised His Name for long
Perhaps, or for the singing-bliss.
   He never sang so good a song
As that which brought the kine to hear,
And the shy hare and timid deer.

(The brother and friend of beast and bird :
   Once, when an oak-bough fell on him
And crushed him, and his cries unheard,
   He swooned, and life went low in him ;
The birds shrieked with such clamour and rout
They brought the human helpers out.)

Oh, but the fields stretched green and glad,
    With stars of gold and stars of white,
No lovelier stars the heaven had,
    The clear pellucid heaven at night :
The low hills tender as the dove
Girdled the bright fields round with love.

The hills were blue, the hills were grey,
    The hills were rosier than the morn.
Thin veils of gold and silver lay
    On emerald fields and fields of corn.
All purple on a sky of glass
A lovelier line there never was.

Down from the Vale of Thrushes came
    That flight of carolling birds, which lit
Where Angus was, and named his name,
    With a clear chorus after it :
And perching on his gown to sing,
They clad him like a feathered thing.

"Sweet, sweet!" the garrulous blackbird
    trilled,
    "Have you not heard, have you not heard
How Angus, more than mortal skilled,
    And more than any singing bird,
Toils in the trenches like a churl ?
The Convent dunghill hath its pearl."

He sang it at the Abbot's ear,
   Who, by his casement in the light,
Painted a missal fair and clear
   With apple-blooms of rose and white.
"Seldom," he murmured, "have I heard
So noisy and so bold a bird."

At last the secret in this wise
   Came to the light. A little lad,
A school-boy with meek, innocent eyes,
   Like those the patient oxen had,
Long strove his difficult task to learn,
And failed; and he was stung with scorn.

One morn, in very evil case,
   Driven from school, he sought the byre,
And flung himself upon his face,
   Sobbing with tearless eyes on fire,
Wishing that he were dead, alas!
Because his world so bitter was.

And while he sobbed, one drew aside
   The straw, and came so stealthily,
The Convent churl, most pitiful-eyed
   For a child's trouble sad to see;
He knelt and whispered words of cheer
And hope and comfort in his ear;

And smoothèd with his fingers rough
  The tangled curls, and touching there,
He seemed to brush the trouble off,
  The dulness that was hard to bear;
He smoothed some tangle of the brain,
And made the difficult lesson plain.

The child climbed out of his kind arms,
  And hied him to the school-house door,
And free from shame and all alarms
  He said his lesson o'er and o'er.
Henceforth, his sluggish brains would be
As clear as crystal verily.

But when his wonderful tale was told,
  They knew, those foolish friars, at last,
Their Convent held the treasure of gold
  Angus, whom for a twelvemonth past
Men sought, then deemed the search was vain,
Since God His gift had taken again.

In a procession they went out,
  The mitred Abbot at their head,
And all the folk, with song and shout,
  Went following down the way they led,
And through the haggard and the barn,
And past the yellowing field of corn.

They found the saint of songs and books
    Feeding his dear kine with sweet grass,
Who turned on him their loving looks;
    And with his brother birds he was.
Seeing, he let the green swathes fall,
And turned his sad face to the wall.

The Abbot knelt and kissed his feet,
    They brought him fine robes to put on,
And fair and costly things to eat,
    A crozier like the sun that shone.
But Angus wept, and sore afeard,
Cast ashes on his hair and beard.

THE LAST WORD.

If you and I were but estranged,
   We might make up another day;
Our hearts, still patient and unchanged,
   Would surely, surely, find the way;
But seeing you are dead, my dear,
There's no more to be said.

If I had loved you all in vain,
   Or your dear love had taken wings,
Why, love that went might come again,
   And life is long for righting things;
But seeing you are dead, my dear,
There's no more to be said.

If I might see you in the street
   To-day, or any day to come
(Sometimes on faces that I meet
   A look of you will strike me dumb) —
But seeing you are dead, my dear,
There's no more to be said.

If any day I woke from sleep
   Might bring a letter with your name,
My heart its patient hope would keep,
   Although your footsteps never came;
But seeing you are dead, my dear,
There's no more to be said.

If we but breathed the same world's air,
   And saw the self-same moon and sun;
If you were living anywhere!
   The rank grass hides your tall gravestone.
And seeing you are dead, my dear,
There's no more to be said.

FAIRY HORSES.[3]

Little Tessie is dreaming still,
   Sitting and singing the self-same song;
The ploughman's coming home from the hill,
   The evening shades are long.

Little Tessie has no fear
   Of lonely fields or lengthening shade,
Crooning low in Boholaun's ear
   The pretty song she made.

Eyes and hair like a gipsy child,
   Heavy lids with a fringe like fur,
The fairies took Shawn Carmody's child
   And in its stead left her.

Russet head to russet weed,
   Tessie's laughing so sweet and low;
She hears below the weed and seed
   The fairy horses go;

Prance, and dance, and champ, and neigh,
    Keeping time to her pretty song;
They stand in golden stalls all day,
    They travel all night long.

If you came at mirk midnight
    Here, where Boholaun stands alone,
You should find a steed of might
    And yellow Boholaun gone.

You should find a steed of might
    Here, where Boholaun fronts the wind,
Soft as silk and milky-white,
    His grey eyes wise and kind.

Kate Carmody stands at her cottage door,
    Large she is, and fair and mild,
Gazing the glooming pastures o'er,
    To find her fairy child.

Tessie heeds not cry or call;
    A fairy ring is on the grass;
Over that circle mystical
    The cattle dare not pass.

Little Tessie has no fear.
    The rooks fly home: she will not stir;
Crooning low in Boholaun's ear
    The song he loves from her.

AUX CARMÉLITES.

Madame Louise sleeps well o' nights,
Night is still at the Carmelites:
    Down at Versailles
The dancers dance, and the violins play.

There's a crucifix on the wall at her head,
And a rush chair set by her pallet bed,
    Stony and hard,
Sweeter than balm or the spikenard.

Daughter of France and the King's daughter,
She hath one poor serge gown to her wear:
    And her little feet
Shall naked go in the wind and sleet.

From things that stabbed her cheek to red
She hath taken her milk-white soul and fled.
    Down at Versailles
The revels go till the break of day.

Sweetly singeth the nightingale
In his screen of boughs while the moon is pale,
    Sweet and so sweet,
That the night-world is faint with it.

The roses dream and the lilies wake,
While the bird of love with his wild heart-break
    Pierceth her dream;
Soft she sighs in the faint moon-beam.

And all night long in the dark by her
An angel sits with its wings astir,
    And his hidden eyes
Keeping the secrets of Paradise.

Madame Louise sleeps well o' nights,
Night is still at the Carmelites:
    Down at Versailles
The dancers dance while the dawn is grey.

VOTIVE OFFERING.

Hearts of silver and of gold
Men had brought in days of old
To Thy shrine for offering,
Symbols of a holier thing.

Lord, Lord, dear, adored!
Take my little candle, Lord;
Through the lights in Paradise
Let my candle please Thine eyes.

Hearts that ache and hearts that break,
Hearts to shatter and remake,
Here before Thy feet are laid,
Where June's roses burn and fade.

Lord, Lord, life is light,
Flame a heart that burns to white;
As this flame mounts steadily,
Draw a heart that turns from Thee.

For a cold heart all its days,
Let my candle tell Thy praise;
For a heart that's ignorant,
Let my candle one hour chant.

Poor my candle is and small,
Yet Thou know'st the thoughts of all:
How my candle saith my prayer
When my feet go otherwhere,—

How one thought I leave behind,
Though my thoughts are hard to bind;
Though I go away, forget,
Thou one hour o'erlookest it.

A STAR'S IMAGE.

A star's track in the clear water ;
    How many a myriad miles away,
The star a world is, vast and fair,
    Gold with eternal day!

Farther than sight or sense can mark,
    Farther than any bird can fly,
Or homeless winds that after dark
    Sail with a lonely cry.

Yet the true water lifts its glass
    Molten to silver, and behold,
Like a pale queen that none surpass
    The far star sees its gold !

Lo then, my heart, a parable !
    Beyond the glory of the star,
A lovelier face than words can tell
    Looks on thee from afar.

Looks on thy face, and thinks to see
    In its unruffled depths made plain,
The Face was marred for love of thee
    With tears of blood and pain.

Yesterday thou hadst woe and stress,
    Yesterday many storms did pass;
Now be thou still, and lift thy face
    The one Star's looking-glass!

RAINY SUMMER.

Are these the fields that were so green
   When last I came this way?
The hawthorn showed no leaves between,
   Stellaria lit the lane that day;
   The birds sang well in May
That now forget to sing—
Did our year's sweet go out with Spring?

Still falls the melancholy rain,
   The tufted grass turns brown;
God's diamond bridge He builds again
   To tell the world she shall not drown;
   Wet mist's the Summer gown,
Scarcely will Robin sing
His lamentation for the Spring.

The wood-dove hath not ceased to mourn,
   The hare's green couch is wet,
In the drenched corn the poppies burn,
   The leaves have many a rivulet;
   But Summer hath not set—
Believe you no such thing—
She weeps for yester-year and Spring.

Let the Spring sleep, I shall not weep,
    She sleeps, and is not dead.
Soon will the wheat grow gold to reap,
    And red fires crown the Autumn's head;
    When all is done and said,
I still have heart to sing,
For every winter tends to Spring.

THE CHAPEL OF THE GRAIL.

O somewhere in this weary world,
   Unseen of eyes like yours and mine,
   There hides a little secret shrine
In a green wood all flower-empearled :
Shrining the Cup that Christ once kissed,
The Cup that held the Eucharist.

A chapel very old and hoar
   Open to Heaven's sweet wind and rain :
   The lancet window's jewelled pane
Spills rose and amethyst on the floor,
And stains with orient dyes and rare
The robe of him who kneeleth there.

Joseph this is who, long ago,
   Gave to the Lord a sepulchre.
   Yea, balsam brought and nard and myrrh,
Gathered from sweetest herbs that grow,
With silkenest sheets that deft hands spin,
To shroud the holy Body in.

Therefore he hath the sacred trust
    To watch and ward the Blessèd Grail,
    While the Earth's centuries fade and fail,
And continents crumble into dust;
He grows not old in heart and limb,
For angels minister to him.

This Chapel where no pilgrims wend
    Hath painted in the wall o' the choir,
    Tall sheaves of wheat whose leaping fire
Endures through Time without an end:
And yellow wheat and purple fruit
Are carven round the altar's foot.

About the porch and window's face
    Ripe grapes in velvet clusters fall,
    The long vines climb the outer wall,
Making green twilight in the place;
And in its jewelled shrine apart
The red Grail pulses like a heart.

Outside are green and solemn woods,
    And overhead the brooding sky,
    Where joyous song-birds flutter and fly.
White doves croon in these solitudes,
And white deer through green arches stray,
Where hares and squirrels are at play.

Heavy with honey flies the bee,
    The lilies plume their silver wings;
    All day a little river sings
Unto its own heart happily;
The tall red roses climb the trees;
There's sudden music on the breeze.

Sometimes an angel goeth down,
    With faint-flushed cheek and glistening curl,
    Lightly with feet of rose and pearl,
And the plucked rainbow in his gown,
Around whose hair the glories play,
Whose wings are apple-blooms in May.

No mortal man might pass unseen
    The sentinels of this Paradise,
    Who pace all day with tireless eyes
And feet the encircling hills of green:
His angels keep with fiery sword
The sanctuary of the Lord.

Yet if a child might travel there,
    (Such an one as your Monica,)
    With just such innocent eyes of awe,
Enaureoled with such amber hair,
The flaming sword might harmless fall,
The way lie open at her call.

But now none finds the secret path ;
   Not Galahad nor Sir Percivale,
   Who once beheld the Blessèd Grail.
In a grey past as old as death :
These wait and dream beside the throne;
And the Lord's secrets are His own.

So in my dream inviolable
   Stand wood and chapel ever and aye,
   A mile away, a world away,
In Earth or Heaven, who shall tell?
Only if one might find that road
It were perchance the path to God.

ALL IN ALL.

Thou knowest, though still I fail and fall,
Thy love is yet mine all in all—
My health, my wealth, my joy, my law,
Yea, and the very breath I draw.

As Peter said, I say the word:
'Thou knowest that I love Thee, Lord!'—
I, stained with more than his disgrace,
And yet so bold before Thy face!

The hills, the vales, my words repeat,—
The solid earth beneath my feet,
The sun, the moon, the stars at even,
Yea, and the listening saints in heaven.

Bear witness now, ye leaping seas,
And all ye woodland palaces,
And Orient lands of spice and scents,
And Northern ice-bound continents:

In this hard heart, so cold and small,
My Lord is still mine all in all;
And if He turn His face away,
A cloud is on the face of day;

And whitest day is blackest night
If I am banished from His sight;
And if afar He lingereth,
My life is living death in death.

A heart so hard, so cold, so small,
What wouldst thou with this heart at all?—
So weak, so poor, so like to stray,
Breaking Thy mandates every day!

And yet, though clogged with sin I be,
I fail not in Thy thought of me;
For on my soul Thyself hast writ
Thy Name, and the sweet grace of it.

And on my soul Thyself canst trace
The pictured likeness of Thy face,
Clear as of old Veronica
Upon the blood-stained kerchief saw.

No true and faithful lover I,
Yet Thy poor lover till I die—
Yea, and past gates of death and birth,
And the lost memory of the earth.

So take Thou me, and, if Thou wilt,
Purge from me all my woe and guilt ;
Show me to angels standing by
Whiter than whitest purity.

See, in Thy hands I lay them all—
My will that fails, my feet that fall ;
My heart that wearies everywhere,
Yet finds Thy yoke too hard to bear.

Yea, with all these my love that still
Loves—for is love not hard to kill ?—
Whose only grace it well may be
Is that it loves so worthily.

TWO IN HEAVEN.

There were two saved souls looking down;
Each had her aureole and gold gown;
    And each the long wings, rosy and sweet,
    Drifting from shoulder to bare feet;
        And each was fair,
With dove's eyes under the pale hair.

So looking down this day and way,
They saw the earth turn, gold and grey;
    And each one sought, 'mid labouring men,
    To see that man she loved again,—
        'Twas many a year
Since the two souls had travelled here.

And one, the elder one, at last
Saw her true lover, holding fast
    His troth to her, his patient faith,
    His love that vanquished time and death
        And pain and fear,
And passed the grave, and leaped to her.

Her heart was glad, her eyes were glad,
And glad the tremulous smile she had;
    Like a small, golden-feathered brood,
    Flew her heart's anthems home to God,
        Singing their song
  Of love that lives though time be long.

Then did she turn, remembering
That younger soul, who with drooped wing
    Leant down; and her dove's eyes were sad.
    And sad the tremulous smile she had.
        "Ah me!" said she;
  "Sister, the earth's mists baffle me!"

The other, looking then, nought said;
She saw the light love comforted,
    She saw the false heart's sorrow done;
    And, gathering then that little one
        In her embrace,
  Covered the troubled eyes and face.

Down through God's Land they go at eve:
The young soul hath forgot to grieve;
    The elder in her gown of white
    Goes dreaming, with her eyes alight,
        Of love and faith,—
  Of faithful Love that conquers Death!

IN IONA.

O 'TIS pleasant in Iona
   Whether in shine or snow!
Grand it is in Iona
   When the north winds blow.
The birds sing sweet in Iona,
   O very sweet and low!
But sore I miss in Iona
   A voice I used to know.

Iona hath the song-birds
   And the hum of the bees,
The distant bark of house-dogs,
   And the wind in the trees.
She hath the singing-cricket,
   And the moan of the seas,
But never the low of cattle
   My homesick heart to ease.

The wee brown cow of Kerry
   Is docile and kind,
The big-framed cow of Leinster
   Is much to my mind,

The wild little cow of the mountains
    Who shall loose or bind?
Sweet is the call of the milkmaid
    Borne upon the wind.

Columba he hath said it—
    " Wherever a cow shall be,
There shall be found a woman,
    Her wiles and witchery.
And in this Holy Island
    May God forbid that she
Should plague with sore temptation
    My holy men and me."

And since the kine are banished
    Heavy my heart doth go,
O sweet it is in Iona
    Whatever wind will blow
But I, the farmer-brother,
    My tears are sad and slow
For the low of the kindly cattle,
    The voice I used to know.

ALL SOULS' NIGHT.

My Love is up in heaven, walking in white,
If but my Love would hear me and come to me
    to-night,
I'd set my door wide open to welcome in my Love,
      To welcome home my Love.

Upon my breast I'd pillow his dark and silken head,
His arms would go about me, his cheek to mine be
    laid,
I should forget my weeping and all my tears and
    pain,
      My heavy tears and pain.

I'd pray my little cock not to crow before day,
I'd pray the dawn to tarry, the mirk midnight to stay,
My pale cheeks would be rosier than any new-made
    bride,
      Than any hour-old bride.

    *   *   *   *   *   *   *

But why is Rory barking as though his heart were
 glad?
All night I heard him keening so mournful and sad,
There's a footstep in the bawn and a hand upon the
 latch,—
   O *whose* hand upon the latch?

Love, and is it you? Love, but you are true,
Tall you are and handsome, the kind Love I knew,
But all in gold and glory, and a crown on your hair,
   A fine crown on your hair.

Crow not, little cock, until the day is come,
Crow not, pretty cock, or my Love must travel home,
And your wings shall be of silver, and gold for your
 crest,
   A gold comb for your crest!

RONDEAU.

Because of you, my only dear,
How radiant grows my atmosphere.
As might a little golden light
Hid in a silence, out of sight,
Fill a dull house with warmth and cheer.

Winter's not cold, or Autumn sere,
But Spring is vernal all the year.
My life goes clothed in bridal white
    Because of you.

You are my sun, my star by night;
My dawn that puts the dark to flight.
What should I be without you, dear?
Without you! Ah, the shade of fear
That chequers all my life's delight
    Because of you.

NOTES.

1. *The Charity of the Countess Kathleen*

This is an authentic folk-story of the West of Ireland, and is perhaps the only instance in legend of one who sold her soul for the Love of God.

2. *The Fairy Foster-mother.*

In Irish fairy-lore the fairies will often steal a mortal woman to nurse their children, as is told here.

3. *Fairy Horses.*

Boholaun, the ragweed, is to the Irish peasant the fairies' horse in daylight disguise.

www.ingramcontent.com/pod-product-compliance
Lightning Source LLC
Chambersburg PA
CBHW030242170426
43202CB00009B/601